Original title:
Pine Forest Prose

Copyright © 2025 Creative Arts Management OÜ
All rights reserved.

Author: Levi Montgomery
ISBN HARDBACK: 978-1-80567-293-7
ISBN PAPERBACK: 978-1-80567-592-1

Ferns and Fables Underfoot

Ferns are whispering tales so spry,
Each leaf a story, don't be shy.
The ground's a stage, the roots all cheer,
For squirrels who prance with a grand premiere.

In muddy shoes, my feet explore,
Treasure maps that lead to more.
A mushroom giggles from its place,
As ants put on a silly race.

Echoes of the Woodland Spirits

The spirits laugh with mischievous glee,
Playing tag with the wind, oh so free.
A crow rolls its eyes at a passing deer,
Who trips on branches—oh dear, oh dear!

Echoes bounce from tree to tree,
With jokes and jests, like a jolly spree.
The owls are hooting one-liners bright,
While foxes grin under the moonlight.

The Stillness Between the Trees

In the stillness, a silence reigns,
But rustling leaves are full of pains.
A pinecone drops with a plop on my head,
I chuckle and think, 'Oh, what have I said?'

The branches sway in a clumsy dance,
Inviting all critters to take a chance.
Branches wave, as if to say,
'Enjoy the mischief, come what may!'

Light's Dance on Mossy Floors

Sunbeams waltz on the soft, green bed,
While shadows prance, a lively spread.
Moss beneath my feet, so cushy and nice,
I might just stay here—add some spice!

A rabbit hops in a tutu rare,
While beetles strut, without a care.
The dance floor spreads from glade to glen,
Up on the logs, and down again!

Conversations Under Conifers

Squirrels chat in high-pitched tones,
While owls wink in feathered zones.
One raccoon spills secrets, oh so sly,
'Now, where's my acorn, oh me, oh my!'

The sun tickles branches, leaves do dance,
A deer prances by, caught in a trance.
'Have you heard about the mossy trend?'
A rabbit replies, 'Only to my friend!'

Glistening Dreams at the Tree Line

Stars twinkle down like fairy lights,
A badger raves about his late-night bites.
'You won't believe, I saw a comet!'
But a hedgehog yawns, 'I'd rather nap on it.'

With moonbeams casting shadows wide,
A group of chipmunks starts to bide.
'Let's make a wish, who dares to leap?'
A voice calls out, 'Only if it's cheap!'

Tangled Vows of the Forest Floor

Fungi whisper to roots below,
Speaking of places they'd like to go.
'Let's take a trip to that stream up high!'
'Only if we don't have to fly!'

Ants march in lines, forming a band,
'We'll conquer the world, take a stand!'
But one slips on dew, what a sight!
'This wasn't the plan, but what a delight!'

The Pulse of Pine Needles

Needles fall like confetti bright,
Each none-too-graceful flight a delight.
A squirrel complains, 'My wig's gone rogue!'
Underneath, a rabbit says, 'Wear the brogue!'

Blades of grass serenade the breeze,
While crickets clap with increasing tease.
'Let's throw a party, invite the bugs!'
A ladybug beams, 'Just bring the hugs!'

Tales Woven in Whispers and Wood

In the grove where squirrels chatter,
A raccoon dances, oh what a matter!
His top hat's askew, such a sight,
He twirls and trips, but his heart's light.

The trees eavesdrop, their laughter flows,
As snails race slowly, that's how it goes.
A deer wears glasses, reading a book,
With giggles that make the whole forest crook.

The owl hoots jokes at the crows' great feast,
While the hedgehogs debate who's the biggest beast.
The wind joins in, it's quite a scene,
As branches sway like a dance routine.

With blossoms laughing upon the boughs,
Each leaf whispers secrets—no one knows how!
In this wood of wonder, humor does play,
Where the jokes are wild and the night turns to day.

The Canvas of Canopied Dreams

Beneath the canopy, shadows twist,
A fox in pjs, I can't resist!
He's threading through the bushes with flair,
While a rabbit hops in his underwear.

The saplings giggle, their roots intertwined,
Pine cones are baseballs, how fun to find!
The sparrows chirp with a comedic spin,
As they sneakily steal from the old bear's den.

Mice throw a party, cheese on a plate,
The dancing is messy, but isn't it great?
The fireflies flash just to shine their shoes,
Bopping around in their sparkling hues.

Each star above winks down in delight,
Watching the woodland revel through the night.
In this painted world of laughter and cheer,
Every soft rustle means fun is near!

The Twilight of the Tall Trees

The tall trees whisper tales at dusk,
Squirrels gossip, while owls just husk.
A raccoon tips his cap, quite neat,
To the moon's glow, a tasty treat.

Branches sway with a silly dance,
Leaves do twirl, if given a chance.
The shadows play peek-a-boo games,
While crickets search for silly names.

Nature's Cloister of Green

In the heart of green, a snail does race,
Over the moss, it's a slow-motion chase.
Frogs croak jokes, oh so absurd,
While butterflies laugh, not saying a word.

Rabbits hop with a jolly tune,
Midday sun, it's quite a boon.
A beaver's grin, quite rogue indeed,
Building a dam, fulfilling a need.

Rituals of the Resinous Heart

The resinous trees host a grand ball,
With sap-dancers twirling, giving their all.
Bugs in tuxedos, such a sight!
Caterpillars shimmy, oh so light.

At twilight, the forest joins in cheer,
A chorus of critters fills the air here.
Even the stones tap their feet,
In this odd gala, life is sweet.

The Quietude of Timbers

In the quiet woods, a twig does snap,
A deer jumps high, nearly a trap.
The trees chuckle, holding their breath,
As nature plays tag, it's a game of stealth.

A log lies down for a snooze so deep,
While owls do gossip, secrets to keep.
The breeze sneezes loudly, trees shake in glee,
In this wooden kingdom, it's funny to see.

Reveries in a Glistening Grove

In a glade where squirrels play,
They plot and scheme all day.
With acorns, they trade and barter,
While birds gossip like a starter.

A raccoon with a mask so sly,
Steals snacks as passersby sigh.
The trees above laugh and stand,
Whispers of mischief, oh so grand.

Mushrooms giggle from their spots,
Poking fun at tangled knots.
A frog joins in with a leap,
While rabbits plot secrets to keep.

The breeze carries laughter far,
As critters dance beneath a star.
In this grove, jesters abound,
Nature's circus, famously crowned.

Trails of Twisted Thoughts

Wandering paths that twist and bend,
Ideas bounce like a lively friend.
Each step brings a chuckle and quirk,
Every shadow hides a smirk.

A squirrel with a suspicious glare,
Steals nuts with style, without a care.
A moose in a hurry trips and falls,
While mockingbirds echo his calls.

Tangled roots like tangled minds,
Play tricks on weary, wandering kinds.
Daisy chains made of puns and jokes,
The trees shake their heads at these folks.

Oddities in nature's grand embrace,
Life's a comedy at a lively pace.
With laughter light as a feathered cap,
Embrace the giggles, take a nap.

Beneath the Arching Branches

Under canopies where shadows loom,
Ideas sprout like flowers in bloom.
A chipmunk juggles with glee so bright,
While ants march on in a silly plight.

A brave little snail moves with finesse,
Deciding it's time to don a nice dress.
Beetles debate who's fastest today,
As lightning bugs light up the play.

Branches overhead take silly shapes,
Like grandpa's stories from old escapes.
The sun peeks in with a teasing grin,
Nature's sense of humor drawn from within.

With laughter sprinkled through the air,
Twisted branches tease without a care.
Beneath the green, let joy well up,
As humor spills from nature's cup.

Solace in the Pine Scented Air

In a verdant realm, smells so divine,
With fragrant whispers like sweet wine.
A bear in shades, lounging with ease,
Contemplates life while munching on peas.

The woods play tricks, shadows vie,
A raccoon winks a knowing eye.
With laughter echoing off every trunk,
Even the grumpiest tree is punked.

Chirpy birds throw a feathery bash,
As giggles follow in a splendid flash.
The saplings shimmy, and the branches sway,
Nature's humor brightens the day.

So fill your lungs with that scented cheer,
Let chuckles linger, never fear.
In the woods where wisdom is sly,
Life's too funny for a serious sigh.

Layers of Lichen and Lore

In shades of green, they slyly creep,
Stories hidden, secrets deep.
They laugh at trees, their knotted stunts,
While mossy cushions host picnic fronts.

The old oak chuckles, leaning low,
While mushrooms dance in a quirky show.
A beetle slips, a laugh escapes,
Those lichen layers round the drapes.

A squirrel mocks with a cheeky flick,
As shadows play their magic trick.
Who knew the woods had such a flair?
With every twist, there's laughter to share!

So when you wander, pause and peek,
At all the whimsy life can speak.
From lichen tales to rooty jest,
The forest loves its playful quest.

Forgotten Paths of the Woodland

Once a path with hints of fun,
Now a jigsaw, lost and done.
A raccoon's party where roots entwine,
And squirrels gossip about the wine.

Twisted branches, a knock-kneed trail,
Where shadows dance and whispers wail.
Take a step, you might just trip,
On tales of acorns and a tiny blip.

Old stones grumble in mossy coats,
While owl-laughter in trees promotes.
The ghosts of travelers shake their heads,
As you weave through the gnome-like threads.

So come and stroll, if you dare,
In this woodland of whimsy, take a share.
For every stumble, there's a tune,
Lost in laughter, under the moon.

The Scent of Earth and Sun

A waft of humor in the bright air,
Rooted giggles, everywhere.
Bumblebees bounce with a buzzing grin,
While daisies gossip, where to begin.

Sunlight spills on a leafy throne,
Mistaken identities grow on their own.
A daffodil whispers to the breeze,
'You think you're funny? Just wait, please!'

Loamy laughter fills the glade,
Where jokes are played, and pranks are laid.
Nature's perfume, a playful jest,
Each scent a giggle, each bloom a quest.

So breathe it in, this earthy muse,
Laughter blossoms, you'll hardly lose.
Let sunshine tickle every wing,
And revel in the joy that nature brings.

Rustling Tales of Nature's Breath

Leaves chuckle softly in playful sway,
As breezes tease them throughout the day.
A fox scampers, leaving footprints neat,
While saying hi to the beetle fleet.

Whispers swirl like candy floss,
Hidden critters seem to gloss.
The wise old owl hoots a punchline sweet,
As the woodland burst in cheerful beat.

Frogs croak verses from the bog,
While a hedgehog hosts a loggy jog.
Laughter echoes through sapling stands,
Creating joy with green-filled hands.

So wander here, lend an ear,
To rustling tales that bring you cheer.
Nature's breath, a comic twist,
In every nook, let laughter persist!

The Grotto of Glowing Moss

In the grotto where the mosses glow,
A rabbit sneezed, causing quite a show.
The mushrooms giggled, their caps tilting high,
As the critters danced beneath the night sky.

A hedgehog tripped on a pebbled stone,
He rolled away, squeaking, 'I'm not alone!'
The fireflies flickered like stars in a race,
While frogs croaked laughter, oh, what a place!

In corners shady, with laughter and glee,
The forest critters held a wild jubilee.
They tossed acorns, trying to score,
While a squirrel claimed, 'I'm the acorn lore!'

Yet when the sun broke, their fun would retreat,
With yawns and stretches, they'd shuffle their feet.
Tomorrow awaits with more jokes to share,
In the grotto where all, leave their worries bare.

Reflections of a Whispering Grove

In a grove where secrets do softly seep,
Trees gossip loudly while creatures peep.
A raccoon with glasses searched for a snack,
He found a big pie, and he knew it was cracked!

The squirrels debated if it's best to share,
Or take the sweet pie and forget the fair.
While owls maintained their wise, lofty stare,
But couldn't resist joining in the dare!

A deer told a tale of a cat in the hat,
Who danced with a mouse and challenged a bat.
The vines giggled low, entwined in the fun,
As laughter erupted; the day had begun!

Yet dusk brought them quiet, as stories fade,
With soft, playful whispers and memories made.
Tomorrow erupts with more tales to find,
In the grove where the whispers are more than kind.

Remnants of Forgotten Memories

Among the fallen leaves, treasures remain,
A cap with a bell, a shoe with no gain.
Beneath twisted roots, laughter still rings,
Of picnics and pranks from long-ago springs.

A squirrel found change from an age long past,
He squeaked, 'I'm rich!' though he ran away fast.
The wind laughed along, rustling old hair,
While shadows played games; oh, what a fair!

Once a bear danced to a silent tune,
Till a big heavy branch made him swoon.
He lay on the ground, pretending to snore,
While the critters just chuckled, 'Let's see him encore!'

As twilight descended, stories would weave,
Of the things that they lost but would never leave.
In remnant-filled memories, the laughter stays,
In the heart of the woods where silliness plays.

The Heartbeat of the Hollowed Earth

In the heart of the earth, a tickling beat,
Where moles spin tales of mischief so sweet.
They burrow in circles, then pop up to tease,
While badgers clap paws, and dance with the breeze.

A beetle adorned in a shiny new hat,
Strolled by the gopher, who shouted, 'What's that?'
As laughter erupted across plush green land,
The echoes of fun were the finest grandstand.

Rabbits played tag with an old, lazy tortoise,
While he rolled his eyes, 'I'll win, mind your hocus!'
But as dusk settled in, the giggles would soar,
With shadows that danced and begged for encore.

When nighttime would hush both wood and the floor,
In the heartbeat of earth, fun would explore.
Tomorrow awaits with more tricks in store,
In the hollowed earth where laughter will soar.

Solitude in the Solstice Woods

In woods where shadows play,
A squirrel steals my snack away.
I ponder life in quiet cheer,
While trees conspiring snicker near.

The sun hangs low, it's time to prance,
I trip and roll—a funny dance.
A chipmunk laughs, I hear its cheer,
My dignity is not quite clear.

Branches wave with gentle tease,
Whispering secrets in the breeze.
I join their joy, I can't resist,
Who knew my peace would come to this?

Twilight brings a quirky end,
Barking at stars, I call a friend.
In solitude, the woods rejoice,
Nature chuckles, it's lost its voice.

Resins and Reveries

Amidst the trees with sticky sap,
I find a cozy spot to nap.
I wake to find a bird on me,
It sings out loud, as proud can be.

With every rustle, giggles rise,
As pine cones plummet from the skies.
They land like hats upon my head,
I laugh aloud, I'm quite misled.

In dreams, I squirrel, I dance and twirl,
The forest floor, my stage, my world.
But branches crack, a sudden crash,
A raccoon joins, we make a splash!

Under the boughs of scented peace,
I share my snacks—a wild feast!
Each nut a treasure, each laugh a cure,
In this odd realm, I feel so sure.

The Green Cathedral's Embrace

In my green church, the rafters sway,
As sunlight streams through foliage play.
The pews are moss, the choir birds,
I join their hymn, forget the words.

A woodpecker, my drummer shy,
A laughing oak, the priest nearby.
They chuckle softly, stories told,
Of acorns lost and legends bold.

With every breeze, a twist of fate,
A bushy tail, no time to wait.
I chase a shadow, I slip and slide,
The laughter echoes, I cannot hide.

In this chapel of green delight,
Where laughter's tune is day and night.
I find my joy, I find my place,
Under the trees' warm embrace.

Sylvan Secrets Unveiled

Beneath the leaves, I hear them speak,
The trees have secrets, oh so weak.
A whisper here, a giggle there,
Nature's jokes are everywhere.

I seek the truth in twisted roots,
While owls discuss their silly hoots.
A raccoon steals my sandwich fair,
He grins and darts without a care.

The sun peeks through, a cheeky light,
As shadows play, they spark delight.
I trip on vines and crash to ground,
The forest shakes with laughter sound.

Each rustling leaf seems to conspire,
To keep my spirit, high and higher.
In sylvan realms where laughter flows,
I find my heart, where humor grows.

Tales Between the Twisted Cracks

Among the trees, where shadows play,
Squirrels gossip all day.
With acorns flying, a nutty spree,
Even the mushrooms giggle with glee.

A bunny hops in, all full of cheer,
Wearing a hat made of fern, oh dear!
The crows all laugh, throwing seeds so fine,
Inventing games that seem quite divine.

When the wind whispers, the branches sway,
It's a dance-off, come join the ballet!
A critter parade, dressed to impress,
Nature's carnival, no room for stress.

So listen close, to the secrets they share,
Woodland antics, beyond compare.
Life here is silly, with fun to unfold,
In this wonderland, let laughs be told.

Assembly of Ancient Giants

Tall and proud, the old ones stand,
Whispering tales of this wild land.
One nudges another, 'Did you see that?'
A raccoon in glass, wearing a hat!

The owls convene, a night-time crew,
Debating loudly their latest view.
One thinks the moon is cheese, divine,
While another insists it's simply a sign.

Down below, the rabbits conspire,
Planning a heist for the woodland choir.
With carrots in hand, they giggle and plot,
The funniest heist, oh what a thought!

But the ancient giants, wise and tall,
Watch the chaos with amusement for all.
In their shade, the antics unfold,
A comedy show, if truth be told.

The Soliloquy of Shaded Places

In glades so dim, where shadows creep,
The flowers gossip, secrets to keep.
A butterfly jokes with a bumblebee,
'That flower's opinion is quite silly!'

The ferns sway gracefully in the breeze,
While lizards sunbathe with remarkable ease.
One tells a tale of a foggy night,
When a lost snail became quite the sight!

Mice reminisce, under mossy wraps,
About the time they trapped some naps.
With cheese so big, and dreams so grand,
Their scheming gets a bit out of hand.

With shadows dancing and laughter near,
These shaded places bring joy and cheer.
So if you wander, stay a while,
Join the fun, and leave with a smile!

Whispers of the Woodland Muse

The trees gossip softly to the tune,
Of the silliest things they might've seen soon.
A raccoon with shades, strutting around,
Waving to all, making quite a sound!

A deer in shoes, prancing with flair,
While the bushes snicker, who'd dare to share?
The chipmunks chuckle at their own jokes,
In this woodland world, full of quirky folks.

As twilight falls, the fireflies blink,
Like stars that come down just to drink.
They twirl and they swirl in a merry dance,
Inviting all critters—come take a chance!

So listen intently to their merry song,
In this forest realm, where you belong.
With laughter abounding and joy in the air,
The woodland muse invites you to share!

A Symphony of Swaying Boughs

In the grove where treetops dance,
Branches sway, a silly prance.
Squirrels jiggle, acorns fall,
Nature's rhythm, a wacky call.

Birds in coats of colors bright,
Squawk a tune that feels just right.
Woodpeckers tap a fun parade,
Every critter's in the trade.

Sunbeams sneak through leafy halls,
Tickling trunks with golden calls.
As laughter bounces off the bark,
The trees reply with joyful lark.

So next time you roam the green,
Join the dance, if you're keen.
With boughs that sway, the fun won't end,
A symphony with every friend.

Guardians of the Ancient Woods

Tall sentinels with faces wise,
Watch as trouble flutters by.
Chipmunks racing, giggling loud,
While shadows stretch, they form a crowd.

Nuts and leaves—a tasty feast,
Who knew that nature was a beast?
The guardians chuckle, share a smile,
While deer prance off in silly style.

Mice throw parties near the roots,
In tiny hats and velvet boots.
As owls hoot their gossip loud,
The forest roars, a comic crowd.

So if you wander where they stand,
Be sure to laugh, just like they planned.
Join the joke, share a pun,
In these woods, the fun's just begun!

Moonlit Murmurs Among the Pines

At night, when stars begin to peep,
The shadows dance, while critters leap.
Moonbeams glow on every lawn,
And giggles follow the mellow dawn.

Foxes share the latest buzz,
"Did you hear what's happened thus?"
The hoot of owls, sweet serenade,
With rustling leaves, the jokes are made.

The crickets chirp and break the news,
While fireflies paint in neon hues.
Starlight winks, a glimmering tease,
It's a comedy, if you please.

So if you roam beneath the moons,
Join the laughter, sing the tunes.
Find the joy 'neath branches fine,
In moonlit murmurs, all align.

The Language of Falling Needles

As needles drop, they speak in codes,
Whispers soft on winding roads.
A tickling touch upon your shoe,
Footsteps giggle, how about you?

Sprinkled down, they form a path,
Underfoot, they spark a laugh.
With every crunch, a joyful tease,
Nature's humor, sure to please.

Critters gather, ears alert,
A comedy show, and not a hurt.
Squirrels debate the best of snacks,
While raccoons plan their midnight hacks.

So stroll along this tiny stage,
With falling needles, turn the page.
In every step, find joy so real,
Nature's chuckle—a grand appeal.

Hushed Harmonies in the Shade

In the shade where whispers play,
Squirrels argue over seeds each day.
Birds sing out in comical tunes,
Chasing shadows, dodging afternoon moons.

A raccoon in a hat asks for a snack,
While trees giggle, leaning back.
Beneath the branches, laughter swells,
Nature's jokes, a tale it tells.

Woodpeckers tap in rhythmic cheer,
Making music that's always near.
And ants march straight with serious glee,
Composing a band of tiny spree.

With every rustle and playful cheer,
It's a comedy show, so come and steer!
In this leafy hall, senses ignite,
Laughter echoes till the fall of night.

Time's Embrace in the Twisted Roots

Roots twist like dancers on a stage,
In their embrace, they write a page.
Old trees gossip with a footnote,
As the wind whispers, 'Take a funny quote!'

The branches bend in a game of tug,
While beetles partake in a tiny hug.
A wise owl naps, dreaming of cheese,
He snores softly, troubling no leaves.

As time meanders, shadows sway,
The ants hold a race, 'First one to play!'
Tick-tock, says the clock on a tree,
Squirrels laugh at its lack of glee.

Each gnarled root holds tales untold,
Of forest capers, both bold and cold.
So sit a while, let giggles unfurl,
In laughter's embrace, joy spins and twirls.

Twilight Chronicles of the Canopy

As dusk falls soft, the stories embark,
From treetops high, they make their mark.
Fireflies write letters in the air,
While bats practice their aerial flair.

A deer reads a joke from the moon's bright glow,
The stars giggle, 'We already know!'
Old branches creak as if trying to chat,
'This forest life is one fine spat!'

Frogs in tuxedos croak out their plight,
'Who took the snacks? It wasn't polite!'
Chirping crickets join the merry tune,
While owls roll dice with a sparkly raccoon.

In twilight's soft lens, antics unwind,
With each rustle, new jokes combined.
As laughter echoes through the shaded glen,
The forest laughs its best, again and again.

Nature's Ink on a Silvan Scroll

On a scroll of leaves, the tales are writ,
Of foxes and badgers, all having a fit.
They gather 'round to share how they fell,
In hilarious ways, oh, how they gel!

A porcupine dances, spines all ablaze,
As rabbits cross paths in a dizzying daze.
With giggles and snickers, they whirl and twirl,
In joyous narratives, their laughter unfurls.

The brook chuckles softly, a trickling jest,
'The fish tell tales of things that are best!'
Mushrooms nod knowingly, sprouting wise cracks,
As the sun dips lower, and night slowly packs.

So let's scribe together under canopies wide,
Where nature's ink flows, and silliness guide.
In every turn, we find joy to extol,
In the heart of the grove, stories fill every hole.

Starlit Secrets in Green Embrace

In the dark, critters dance,
Squirrels in a prance.
Moonlight on their tails,
Whiskers twitch, and giggles sail.

Tree branches whisper low,
"Did you see that show?"
A badger steals a pie,
Underneath the sparkling sky.

Down on the ground, owls hoot,
Laughing at a sneaky fruit.
One tree said, "What a night!"
A raccoon strumming in delight.

With branches held up high,
"Who left the nuts to dry?"
Sawdust dreams in the night,
For creatures lost in flight.

Revelations Under Bark and Bough

Underneath a timbered tale,
A fox told a funny fail.
"Chased my tail and rolled away,
Thought it was a bright buffet!"

Tree trunks giggled at his plight,
"How do you lose in broad daylight?"
A wise old owl rolled his eyes,
"Only fools fall for those lies!"

Beetles formed a little band,
Playing songs across the land.
One slipped on a fallen leaf,
Managed to dance with no belief!

Boughs began to sway and swing,
As wind chimed in to sing.
Nature laughed without a care,
As laughter filled the open air.

A Canopy of Dreams

Beneath the leaves, a bug did roam,
"Hey, where's your comfy home?"
He found a cozy nook so neat,
Only to trip on his own feet!

A chattering chipmunk joined in,
"Got snacks? Can I begin?"
"With all this fluff, we feast,"
Came the cry of a raucous beast!

A squirrel jumped from twig to twig,
"Life in the trees — oh so big!"
He missed a branch, took a dive,
Pretended it was all a jive.

The moon peeked through the green,
Sparkling like it's never seen.
Nature giggled, hearts in bloom,
As dreams twirled in the nighttime gloom.

Mist Where the Pines Meet

Where the shadows come to play,
A rabbit's lost — can't find his way.
"Is this the path or just a prank?"
"Those bushes tickled, what a rank!"

Fog rolled in like a jolly ghost,
Morning jokes were what he'd boast.
"Can I play hide and seek?" he squeaked,
But mist just laughed, and then it peeked!

Geese quacked, sharing quite a jest,
"Found a hat! It's better than the rest!"
A wandering deer joined the fun,
"Let's dance! Come on, everyone!"

Mirth echoed through branches high,
As echoes paired with a sigh.
In the mist where laughter breeds,
Nature's the best at planting seeds!

Whispers Among the Needles

In the woods, squirrels conspire,
Chasing each other, never tire.
A feathered choir sings loud and clear,
While acorns roll, we share a cheer.

A tree stump stands with a silly grin,
As if it knows where the fun begins.
Oh, what mischief the critters share,
In a land where laughter fills the air.

Beneath a Canopy of Silence

Underneath the boughs so wide,
A fox put on a funny slide.
With leaves as wings, it glides with flair,
While badgers giggle without a care.

Fungi dance in a wobbly line,
Mushrooms twirl, feeling divine.
The silent trees sway to the beat,
Nature's jesters, oh so sweet!

Echoes of the Timbered Realm

A raccoon wears a hat from twigs,
Pretending it's a lord of the digs.
With every step, a crunch resounds,
In the echo, laughter abounds.

Squirrels hold meetings up in the trees,
Debating on which nut is the keys.
A wisdom so profound, it seems,
While they nap, inside funny dreams.

Shadows of the Evergreen Giants

In shadows deep, a dance unfolds,
Where ancient trees play pranks so bold.
A pinecone slips, takes a little fall,
And giggles rise, the woodland's call.

The giants sway like tipsy fools,
While chipmunks chuckle, breaking rules.
Underneath, the laughter roars,
As nature's jesters open doors.

Elixirs of Earth and Ether

In the woods where squirrels plot,
Nuts are hidden, why not a shot?
Mushrooms dance on the forest floor,
Wondering if they'll start a store.

Bees debate who stole the jam,
In their hive, it's quite the scam.
A rabbit sneezes, all does flee,
Was that a sound of glee or a plea?

The owls hoot, their eyes bling wide,
Should've known, they're not good at hide.
Acorns drop a rhythm in time,
A beat that leaves squirrels in their prime.

Nature's mix in every nook,
Crafting laughter like a book.
Here we frolic, whimsy in air,
Fun in the twigs, without a care.

Treading the Twining Trails

Along the paths where shadows dart,
A lizard's dance is a goofy start.
Beneath the leaves, a chorus sings,
Melodies from earthy flings.

A hedgehog prances with style rare,
Sporting a haircut, oh beware!
The turtles chuckle, racing slow,
In this green realm, time's always low.

Branches twist like painted mind,
Trying hard but can't unwind.
The wind chimes in, with jokes galore,
Whispered secrets, nature's lore.

Mushrooms laugh at their tall trees,
"Stand up straight!" they tease with ease.
As we tread these twining trails,
Fun's the compass that never fails.

Flickers of Life in the Darkened Wood

At dusk, the critters start to glee,
Glowing bugs have a disco spree.
Branches wiggle, with moonlit cheer,
Frogs croak tunes while deer lend an ear.

The shadows play hide and seek,
A raccoon's antics reach their peak.
Squirrels with acorns, all in a race,
Chasing their tails in a jocular chase.

The whispers of trees, secrets they keep,
A quiet giggle as shadows leap.
Night owls chuckle at stealthy mice,
"Can't you see? You're not very nice!"

Amidst the dark, the joy ignites,
In this wood of fanciful sights.
Nature's whimsy, an endless book,
Flickers of life, come take a look!

Lingering Lights in Leafy Sanctuaries

In sanctuaries where sunlight weaves,
The rabbits dance in leafy sleeves.
Bubbles of laughter float in the breeze,
Tickled by foxes with utmost ease.

Butterflies gossip on petal seats,
Planning a soirée with scrumptious treats.
With nectar glasses, they toast and sway,
Nature's party, hip-hip-hooray!

Investigating angles, a deer strolls through,
Hoping for snacks that are tasty and new.
Chirps and giggles fill the space,
In this leafy world, there's no race.

Every nook spills with light and cheer,
Wrapping around, it draws us near.
Lingering laughs in the gentle shade,
In these places, silliness is made.

The Breath of Ancient Pines

In the woods where the trees all sway,
The squirrels plot schemes in a playful way.
They toss acorns with glee, a fine little sport,
While the deer take a nap, their dreams all court.

Mossy carpets and mushrooms abound,
Twirling branches make a soft, funny sound.
The birds sing a tune, off-key but sweet,
While the foxes gather to dance on their feet.

As twilight creeps in, the shadows grow long,
A chorus of laughter; they all sing along.
The owls roll their eyes, they've had quite enough,
As echoes of giggles make the night tough.

So here in the woods, let us all play,
With nature's wink, we'll frolic and sway.
For in every rustle and every breeze,
Lies the humor of life among ancient trees.

Echoes of the Evergreen

In the glen where the green giants stand,
A raccoon steals snacks, oh isn't it grand?
With a lopsided grin, he makes quite the mess,
As the chipmunks all giggle, they couldn't care less.

The ferns wave their fronds to a tune of delight,
While the rabbits throw parties that last through the night.

They hop and they twirl, with such carefree flair,
While the owls roll their eyes, pretending not to care.

As evening descends, the critters unite,
The crickets start chirping, they're ready to bite.
The frogs jump in sync with a croak and a splash,
While the turtles just laugh, taking life slow with a dash.

Oh what a ruckus, what joy fills the air,
In the green and the laughter, we banish despair.
For the trees stand as guardians, wise and serene,
While nature's own jesters bring joy to the scene.

Symphony of the Silvan

In the heart of the grove where the laughter rings,
A raccoon strums branches, pretending he's king.
With a wink and a nod, he plays on his own,
While the squirrels gather 'round, they're starting to moan.

Beneath every leaf, there's a tale taking flight,
With critters creating their own minor plight.
A rabbit hops high, claiming he can fly,
While the foxes just chuckle, saying "Oh my, oh my!"

When twilight unfolds, the fireflies glow,
The trees whisper stories to all down below.
The beetles join in for a grand old parade,
As the owls look bemused, thinking "Aren't they too played?"

So here in the thicket, where giggles abound,
Nature's own laughter is forever unbound.
With each rustle and whisper, we join in the fun,
For the woods are a stage, and we're never outdone.

Secrets of the Standing Sentinels

Beneath the tall guards, where shadows play nice,
The critters all gather for an evening of spice.
The chipmunk leads, with its tiny parade,
While the pigeons just coo, thinking they're quite laid.

A squirrel in spectacles reads from a book,
While the rabbits distract with their classic good looks.
As laughter erupts from each twist and the turn,
The tales of the woods keep the critters quite stern.

In the hush of the dusk, they dance on the leaves,
While the moon in the sky winks through the eaves.
With a hop and a skip, they join hands in rings,
As the trees murmur softly, sharing secret things.

So join in the revels 'neath the canopy bright,
With giggles and fun, we weave laughter and light.
For in every whisper, there's a chance to be free,
Surrounded by nature, in sweet jubilee.

Sentinel Shadows in Autumn's Glow

Tall trees wear jackets of gold,
While squirrels sneak snacks that are bold.
Leaves whisper secrets of laughter,
As critters run, chasing disaster.

Sunlight dances through branches high,
Beneath the boughs, a rabbit sighs.
He's plotting mischief, quite a show,
While acorns drop with a plucky throw.

Chirping birds critique the scene,
A feathered jury, full of keen.
They laugh as the ground starts to dance,
Every leaf joins in, a merry prance.

As shadows stretch and giggles blend,
In this wild glade, there's no end.
Autumn's glow, a playful jest,
In this realm, nature's at its best.

The Tapestry of Moss and Memory

Where moss weaves tales of sleep and play,
Fungi pop up in a cheeky display.
A snail contests a snail's pace race,
With laughter echoing all over the place.

Old logs hold wisdom in their grain,
Whispering jokes of sunshine and rain.
While frogs croak punchlines, so absurd,
Swaying along on each friendly word.

Beneath a patchwork of vibrant hues,
A sleepy fox snores, dreaming of shoes.
He wakes to realize it's all in his head,
And curls up again, ignoring what's said.

Memories stick like glue in the air,
With each giggle, it lightens the flare.
This tapestry, stitched with a laugh,
Reveals the soft heart of nature's staff.

A Journey Through Aromatic Layers

In fragrant layers, scents collide,
As mushrooms grin and fungi abide.
Breezes hum tunes of ages past,
While bushy tails dart by so fast.

Each footstep crunches a savory treat,
As ants march on with nimble feet.
They carry crumbs like hefty kings,
Dancing around with their quirky swings.

Herbs and spices mingle in flirt,
Sage whispers softly, cautious and alert.
A wayward bee buzzes a tune,
In a garden of chaos, under the moon.

Rich aromas weave tales old and new,
In this aromatic circus, wild joy ensues.
With each breath taken, laughter's found,
In the layers where nature spins round.

The Breath of the Silent Grove

In a grove where silence loves to play,
Even the winds choose to sway.
Branches crack jokes that leaves don't tell,
As shadows giggle, casting their spell.

A hedgehog ponders life's great schemes,
Why not roll into pies and creams?
While rabbits throw unplanned parade,
With carrots and muddles in a grand charade.

The hush is loud, yet laughter's near,
Spirits wander without a fear.
Every rustle is a prankster's glee,
In the silly whispers of this calm spree.

As the day bows down, the jokes take flight,
Under the stars, everything's light.
In this silent grove, with joys that blend,
Nature's humor knows no end.

The Starlit Serenade of the Woods

Under the stars, the trees sway high,
Frogs croak ballads, oh me, oh my!
Squirrels jive, with nuts in tow,
While owls hoot tunes, putting on a show.

Moonlit nights bring a waltz so bright,
The shadows dance in sheer delight.
A chipmunk tries a solo feat,
Accidentally trips on its own two feet!

Fireflies flicker, a disco ball,
"Insect or dancer?" we wonder, and all.
The crickets form a band that's bold,
As laughter echoes, their antics unfold.

So here we sing 'neath the twinkling glow,
In a woodland giggle where joy will grow.
The starlit serenade, oh what a sight,
Where fun and nature blend every night!

Shadows of Spruce and Fir

In the shadows sleek, where trees align,
A bear wears shades, sipping on brine.
Hey there, buddy, are you on a spree?
Or just lost your way from a picnic spree?

A rabbit hops with such flair and grace,
Wearing a bowtie, matching its face.
Squirrels gossip, chattering fast,
About that raccoon who stole their last!

The shadows tease with every gust,
"Is that a stick? Or post-party dust?"
Each rustle sounds, like a joke setup,
With nature's chuckle filling each cup!

And as twilight laughs, the sun dips low,
Creatures gather for the evening show.
In shadows of spruce and fir so grand,
Nature's comedy club, a stellar strand!

Meandering Through the Misted Pines

Wander through mist where giggles float,
A porcupine "pricks" with a witty quote.
"Life's like a thorn," it quips with a grin,
"Better not sit down, or you'll take it on the chin!"

Hens laugh at crows with their messy style,
"Your feathers look wild – go comb for a while!"
A fox strolls by with a swagger so neat,
"I'm sly, I'm cool, and I snack on sweet treats!"

In the sway of trees, a chorus begins,
Mice wearing hats, joining in with their sins.
"Who stole the cheese? Let's have a debate!"
All while the owls just stand at the gate.

Through misted pines, the chuckles ignite,
A woodland jaunt that feels just right.
Each rustle and giggle, a magical sign,
As laughter echoes, we feel so divine!

Whispers of the Woodland Whimsy

In the woodland turns, a rabbit goes,
Wearing a crown made of daisies and bows.
"Royal in my realm, don't dare to scoff!"
They twirl with style, then suddenly cough!

A chipmunk with glasses, scholarly grace,
Reads a book titled "How to Win a Race."
"Step one," it whispers, "always look spry,
Unless there's a hawk; then just say goodbye!"

The trees are giggling, branches sway low,
As winds whisper secrets that only they know.
"Did you see the fox? It tripped on a vine!"
Nature's eternal comedy, sparkling and fine.

With whimsy surrounding, the sun dips and glows,
The woodland's a stage where laughter just flows.
In whispers and chuckles, the evening unfolds,
In a world of delight, where pure joy beholds!

The Dance of Dappled Light

Sunlight skips through leafy shades,
Casting shapes where squirrel parades.
A rabbit hops, then strikes a pose,
In the glimmering, ticklish close.

Twigs crackling like a joke,
Joyful whispers, nature's poke.
Frogs croak in a croaky cheer,
As the breeze throws giggles near.

Chasing shadows, a dog prances,
Bumping trees in silly dances.
A butterfly flutters, wings aflame,
Twisting, twirling, wild and tame.

Laughter echoes through the trees,
Carried by the humming breeze.
In this light, we play and sing,
Among the giggles that we bring.

Fragrance of the Wildwood

Whiffs of mystery, oh so sweet,
With mushrooms dancing at our feet.
A skunk passes, gives a wink,
Leaving us all to stop and think.

The wild berries burst with glee,
Sticky smiles, they're good, you see!
Ants march on a picnic spree,
Taking crumbs someday to be free.

A squirrel's mask, a comedic thief,
Stealing snacks with utter disbelief.
The fresh aroma of piney pies,
Makes us chuckle, oh how time flies!

As the sun dips, shadows blend,
Nature's tales seem to extend.
We gather 'round, a feast of fun,
In the aroma that's just begun.

A Tapestry of Twisting Trunks

Twisted trunks in silly lines,
Hugging grasses, planting signs.
A knotty tree tells tales of yore,
While tangled roots beg us for more.

Lizards bask on branches high,
Sunbathing in the bright blue sky.
A woodpecker knocks, a rhythmic beat,
As branches sway to a heartbeat treat.

The dance of branches, side by side,
Encouraging composting as we glide.
Laughter bounces back and forth,
In this quirky place of mirth.

A curling vine takes a bow,
Cheering on with a leafy wow.
In every twist, humor hides,
Among the structure where fun abides.

Beneath a Shroud of Verdant Dreams

Beneath the leafy curtains' sway,
Chirpy birds join in the play.
A raccoon juggles acorns round,
While giggles wake the froggy sound.

The ground's a carpet, soft and bright,
A perfect spot for silly fright.
Here, whispers weave like knitted thread,
As funny thoughts bounce in our head.

The shadows twist like a magic spell,
Inviting us into a giggly well.
Woodland creatures, in jest, unite,
As echoes dance in the fading light.

Among the ferns, we lie and dream,
With flickering stars, a glinty beam.
Under the leafy, playful schemes,
Joyful secrets weave our dreams.

A Lyrical Journey Among the Leaves

In a place where squirrels chatter,
And branches do a little dance,
Leaves fall in joyful patterns,
Like nature's silly prance.

A bird starts a karaoke show,
With tunes that make the owls laugh,
The trees sway to and fro,
Joining in on the goofy gaffe.

Dancing mushrooms on the ground,
Whispering secrets in the breeze,
What a funny world we've found,
With laughter echoing through the trees!

So here we wander without care,
With giggles bouncing all around,
In this world of green so rare,
Where joy and whimsy can abound.

Secrets in the Softening Bark

The trees have tales they often tell,
In grooves and knots, they share their plight,
Of critters who dance, oh so well,
Under the silver moonlight.

A gopher's giggle starts the fun,
His home a laughable little mess,
Squeaking loudly he's just begun,
Spreading joy with each address.

Beetles play poker with acorns,
While the frogs judge from the leaves,
Who knew bark held such deep forms?
A place where nonsense never leaves!

So come, let's listen and unwind,
To nature's jests, both wild and sweet,
In this enchanted space we find,
A comical, leafy retreat.

The Magic of the Mossy Path

There's a trail that sings of glee,
With moss that tickles toes,
Rabbits bouncing wild and free,
In a world where laughter grows.

Each step reveals a silly song,
As mushrooms wiggle in delight,
With every hop they sing along,
Turning day into a paling night.

Capers and capers everywhere,
A fox tries to dance but slips,
Rolling down without a care,
While hedgehogs chuckle in their strips.

So wander down this mossy way,
Where joy and jests never part,
In nature's arms we gladly play,
With laughter filling every heart.

Flickering Shadows in Green Sanctuary

In a grove where shadows twirl,
And sunlight flickers like a joke,
A lizard struts with a funny whirl,
Wearing leaves as his bespoke cloak.

The shadows trade their silly puns,
While gnomes sip tea in the shade,
The trees applaud their funny runs,
As if a grand parade is made.

A raccoon sporting a bright bowtie,
Winks at a curious little bee,
Spinning yarns that make us sigh,
In this green sanctuary, oh so free!

So let's embrace this playful place,
Where laughter dances with each breeze,
In nature's wit, we find our space,
Among the rustling leaves and trees.

The Vow of the Verdant

In a patch of green, where the squirrels play,
A trio of trees had much to say.
They vowed to stand firm, never to bend,
Unless a strong breeze chose to offend.

A rabbit remarked, 'You're quite proud, hey?'
The trees swayed a bit, but that was okay.
With humor and grace, they danced to a tune,
While a fox told a joke 'neath the full silver moon.

The sun peeked through leaves, wearing a grin,
As laughter erupted, how silly they'd been.
They giggled and jiggled, their bark all aglow,
The forest would echo—come join the show!

Soon creatures convened for a joyous parade,
Each one with a story that just had to be made.
In the heart of the verdant, laughter rang clear,
Binding them close, without worry or fear.

Cerulean Skies and Verdant Stories

Under skies so blue, 'neath a canopy wide,
Animals gathered, with jokes to confide.
The owl cracked a pun while hanging upside down,
As the badger just snorted, losing his frown.

A tale of a snail that raced with a hare,
Made all chuckle hard, forgetting their care.
The hedgehog rolled in, with quills in a twist,
'It's me against time!' he had boldly insisted.

Squirrels brought acorns—each one a delight,
To bait all the critters and spark their delight.
Tales of survival from nuts and from leaves,
Filled with bizarre but humorous thieves.

When twilight set in, under starlight so bright,
The forest erupted in sheer, silly fright.
With bright lanterns swinging, the stories still flowed,
Laughter and friendship, the sweetest abode.

Harmony on the Hidden Trail

A trail that meanders, oh where could it go?
With hedges that whisper, they put on a show.
A raccoon on a mission, lost in his snacks,
Humor's the treasure that nobody lacks.

The deer in the distance, so elegant, sly,
Trying not to giggle, she glanced at the sky.
And a chipmunk declared, with a cheeky little grin,
'Join me or else, I might just nick your kin!'

They bopped and they twirled, on the carpet of green,
Creating a scene that was simply serene.
With laughter and chatter, they conquered their woes,
Each heart full of music, each friend a hero.

When dusk came to canvas, their tales would replay,
Of mishaps and laughter, come gather and stay.
The hidden trail echoed, a melody bright,
In harmony's arms, they danced through the night.

Essence of the Enchanted Grove

In a grove of delight where the fables run free,
A wild bunch of critters met under a tree.
The bear cracked a joke, rather heavy, you see,
And the atmosphere crackled with whimsical glee.

A wise old tortoise, who wore quite a hat,
Chimed in with a riddle, 'What walks with a spat?'
All pondered aloud, with furrows and frowns,
Until laughter exploded and turned into sounds.

The squirrels soon joined, swinging acorns like stars,
Filling the air with their miniature bars.
Each tale turned to jest, a delightful charade,
While the grove clapped its branches, a flash of parade.

When the moon stood so proud and glimmered with cheer,

The laughter grew louder, no worries, no fear.
In the essence of magic, they found pure delight,
An enchanted adventure on this glorious night.

Paths Among the Verdant Giants

In the woods where trees stand tall,
Squirrels gather, having a ball.
They chitter and scamper, quite a sight,
While I trip over root, what a fright!

Branches wave like hands in cheer,
Inviting me to share their beer.
One tree grumbled, 'Not again!'
I laughed and danced like rain on zen.

Mushrooms giggle underfoot,
As rabbits tap dance, isn't that cute?
The sunlight flickers, making shadows play,
I'm lost in their fun, come join the fray!

Yet off I roam without a map,
Following critters in a silly lap.
I found a frog who croaked with glee,
Said, 'You're a silly human, can't you see?'

Harmony in the Hushed Glade

In the glade where whispers thread,
A chipmunk said, 'You lost your head?'
With acorns piled like winter stock,
He chuckled at my woeful walk.

The fox looked sleek, with style so grand,
While a turtle danced, a slow band.
They sang a tune, a comical plight,
Of berry picking gone wrong that night!

The owls hooted, 'What's all the fuss?',
While bees buzzed in their yellow bus.
Laughter echoed between the trees,
'At least we have the honey, please!'

Nature's laughs blend with the breeze,
While I try hard not to sneeze.
A tumble here, a giggle there,
In this wild choir, who needs a care?

Layers of Leaf and Time

Beneath the canopy, green and free,
The leaves tell secrets, winks from the tree.
One said, 'Stop! Your pants are stuck!'
I wriggled and giggled, out of luck.

The layers of branches like layers of cake,
Every step I take, my shoes misplace.
A parade of ants marched in a line,
'Excuse us, human! We're doing fine!'

The shadows play tricks, make me dance,
While falling leaves give nature a chance.
A lone crow cawed, 'Are you a clown?'
I bowed to him, fell flat on the ground!

Yet laughter rings louder than my blunder,
As squirrels plot, 'Let's give her thunder!'
So here I roam with giggles in mind,
In layers of leaves, true magic I find.

Echoes of the Woodland Spirit

The woodland spirit, a cheeky sprite,
Whispers jokes as day turns night.
With mushrooms as hats, he winks with glee,
'Who needs a mirror? Look at me!'

Trees sway in rhythm, a dance so bold,
While bushes gossip, 'Did you hear what's told?'
They giggle and wiggle, oh what a scene,
Nature's humor, fit for a queen!

A laugh erupts from a bubbling brook,
'The frogs are auditioning; take a look!'
I watched in awe as they jumped and croaked,
A performance done, applause invoked.

In this realm of whimsy, under bright stars,
Laughter is king, and joy's never far.
So tread lightly, dear friend, let worries depart,
In echoes of laughter, you'll find a warm heart.

Reflections in the Pine Needle Puddle

In puddles deep, the trees do stare,
With needle hats, they seem to care.
A squirrel jumps in, with quite a splash,
Making fish jump out, oh what a clash!

The frogs croak loud, in a sing-song way,
While turtles watch, they laugh and play.
The sun peeks down, what a sight to see,
A laughing tree, or maybe just me!

Beneath the leaves, the shadows dance,
Mice prance around in a silly trance.
A raccoon trips on his own two paws,
A forest clown with no applause!

So next time you wander near the glade,
Remember the fun each creature made.
In puddles bright, where giggles rain,
Nature's jesters are never plain.

Guardians of the Gnarled Roots

Beneath the boughs, they twist and turn,
Guardians old, with secrets to learn.
Gnarled roots laughing, in wiggly glee,
They gossip about the buzz of a bee.

A raccoon sneaks by, with snacks to share,
Roots pipe up, 'Hey, can you spare?'
The laughter twists through the earthy space,
As mushrooms chuckle in their cozy place.

The owls hoot jokes in a serious tone,
While the wise old fox stirs up the zone.
"You think you're clever, but check that twig,
It's just a hat for my dance, look big!"

So gather round, where roots entwine,
For nature's jesters are truly divine.
With laughter that tumbles, oh what a sight,
Even gnarled roots know how to ignite!

The Language of Wind and Bough

The wind whispers tales that tickle the leaves,
Boughs bend low, like they're sharing thieves.
"Did you hear that?" one branch starts to trill,
"I once saw a squirrel, who tried to be still!"

A gentle breeze joins in with a hum,
Singing of nut hunts, oh what fun!
The leaves ripple laughter, a rustling crew,
As they plot mischief with a bird or two.

"Let's play a game," the branches shout wide,
"We'll dance with the wind on this joyous ride!"
The air fills with giggles, a sweet serenade,
Nature's own joke, a merry charade.

So listen closely next time you roam,
In whispers and rustles, you'll feel at home.
For in the wind's voice, there's laughter untold,
And secrets of joy that never grow old.

Moonlight on the Forest Floor

The moon casts glow, a spotlight shared,
On critters below, who simply dared.
A badger trips light on his nightly quest,
With a clumsy leap, he's pretty much a jest!

The crickets chirp with comedic flair,
As fireflies twinkle, up in the air.
"Dance on, my friends," the owl gives a hoot,
While hedgehogs roll, in a wobbly suit.

In whirls of laughter, the shadows play,
With raccoons at the helm, leading the way.
They tap dance on leaves with delightful glee,
A midnight ball, who needs a VIP?

So if you stroll beneath silver beams,
Join in on the fun, follow your dreams.
For in moonlit nights, where laughter soars,
The forest lives on, with whimsical roars!

Lullabies of the Windward Trees

In breezy whispers, branches sway,
Squirrels dance, laughing all day.
A crow tells tales of lost acorns,
While the sun plays peek-a-boo with thorns.

The wind hums tunes of ancient lore,
As chipmunks plot, behind each door.
A party's brewing deep in the boughs,
With tree frogs croaking, "Who's got the cows?"

Dancing shadows, laughter they weave,
A secret club, you wouldn't believe!
Underneath a moonlit plight,
Their secret jokes make the night feel bright.

Nature's comedy, wild and free,
Join the jests of the wiggly tree.
Where every rustle and jittering sound,
Makes for laughter, all around.

Conversations with the Canopy

Two owls gossip, wise and sly,
About the squirrel who learned to fly.
A rustling leaf shouts, "Wait for me!"
While ants argue who climbed the tree.

Branches tickle the clouds above,
As they plot a surprise for the dove.
With acorns tossed and plenty of cheer,
Every creature joins in the fun, no fear!

"Watch out," says a raccoon with glee,
"Here comes a squirrel, he's just like me!"
They chuckle loud as the branches bend,
In this leafy talk, there's no end.

Under moonlight, laughter rings clear,
With woodland friends, there's nothing to fear.
So come share secrets, jokes, and some tricks,
With trees that chat and nature's quick picks.

Heartbeats of the Timberline

At timberline where the bravest play,
The bushes giggle in a cheeky way.
A deer shows up with a bowtie neat,
While shadows chuckle on nimble feet.

Breezes carry jokes from bough to bough,
"Why did the pine wear a floppy crown?"
"It thought it was fancy, or so it said,
But simply it's just a tree on its head!"

The groundhogs plot a prank with flair,
"Let's stick pine cones in a bear's hair!"
With echoes of laughter, they eagerly prance,
In nature's theater, they wiggle and dance.

Their hearts beat loud, a playful tune,
'Neath the watchful gaze of the bright full moon.
So join the fun, let your joy unwind,
At the edge of the wild, all laughter aligned.

The Solitude of Silhouettes

In twilight hues, the shadows play,
Silhouettes dance, in a comical sway.
A fox in glasses reads a fine book,
While rabbits gossip in every nook.

The trees point fingers—a game of charades,
As nighttime prowlers start their escapades.
A deer plays shy, with a gentle grin,
While fireflies blink like they've drunk some gin.

Moonlit mischief fills the air,
With owls who squawk, as if they're a pair.
"Did you hear about the chatty pine?
He spills the secrets of every vine!"

Through all the laughter, a mystery thrives,
In the solitude where funny life dives.
Join the silhouettes in their nightly affairs,
Where humor and nature weave through the airs.

www.ingramcontent.com/pod-product-compliance
Lightning Source LLC
Chambersburg PA
CBHW071850160426
43209CB00003B/489